ESSENTIAL **DK** LIFESKILLS

Improving Your Memory

David Thomas

DK Publishing

DK

LONDON, NEW YORK, MUNICH,
MELBOURNE & DELHI

Project Editor Nicky Munro
Senior Art Editor Sarah Cowley
DTP Designer Rajen Shah
Production Controller Mandy Innes
US Editors Margaret Parrish and
Christine Heilman
Managing Editor Adèle Hayward
Managing Art Editor Marianne Markham
Category Publisher Stephanie Jackson

Produced for Dorling Kindersley by

studio **cactus** ©

13 SOUTHGATE STREET WINCHESTER HAMPSHIRE SO23 9DZ

Designer Dawn Terrey
Editor Sue Gordon
Managing Editor Mic Cady

First American Edition, 2003
05 06 07 10 9 8 7 6 5 4

Published in the United States by
DK Publishing, Inc
375 Hudson Street
New York, New York 10014

Thomas, David, 1968-
Improving your memory / David Thomas.
p. cm.--(Essential lifeskills)
Includes index.
ISBN 0-7894-9325-X (alk. paper)
1. Memory. 2. Mnemonics. I. Title. II. Series.

BF371 .T46 2003
153.1'4--dc21   2002031332

Reproduced by Colourscan, Singapore
Printed in China by WKT Company Limited

See our complete product line at
www.dk.com

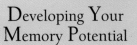

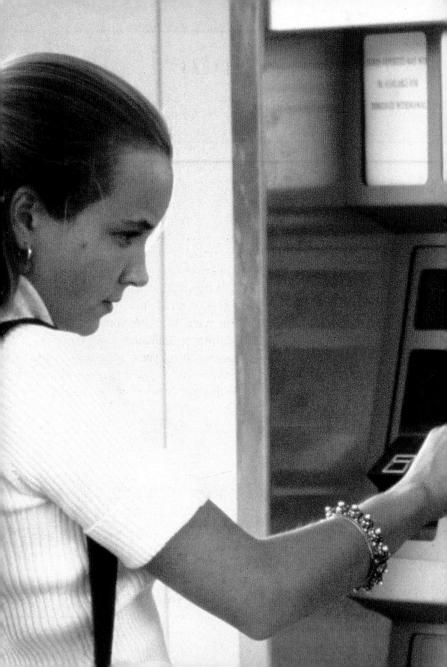

Introduction

Mental performance is fast becoming the key not only to personal and professional success but also to the quality of life. An active, powerful memory is the bedrock of our whole mental performance. Improving Your Memory *takes you on a journey of self-discovery, showing how your memory works, how to develop its full potential, and how to use it effectively in daily life. The memory-training techniques reveal the level to which you can take your performance, and the applications give you an insight into how you can use memory skills in all areas of life. Self-assessment exercises enable you to evaluate your performance. Enhancing your memory's capabilities will boost your confidence, expand your creativity, and improve your performance in day-to-day life, at work, study, and play.*

Understanding Memory

Memory is a human faculty that is shrouded in mystery. Understanding how it works will both inspire you and enhance your ability to use it to its full potential.

What Is Memory?

Memory defines us as individuals. Each of us has unique and irreplaceable memories from a very early age. Memory also enables us to manage our daily lives. Only when memory starts to fail us do we realize how central it is to our identity.

FOCUS POINTS

● Make good use of your memory to get more out of life. Our basic quality of life is rooted in memory.

▲ **Anticipating the future**
When you look forward to something with pleasure—for example, a vacation at the beach—you may do so because you have happy memories of similar occasions in the past.

MEMORY AND INDIVIDUALITY

Your memory, to a large extent, makes you who you are. It is not simply a database of information: your memories influence your outlook on life and consequently your response to events. New experiences are shaped by your memory. Your reaction to an event is based on previous experiences of something the same or similar.

WHY MEMORIES DIFFER

One person's recollection of an event is likely to differ widely from another person's memory of the same event. This is because, unlike a photographic image, a memory is not imprinted precisely on the mind. A memory is made up of pieces of information taken in and processed by the brain in a way that is unique to each individual. Your recollection of an event will always be in the context supplied by the other memories and information that are already stored in your brain.

FOCUS POINTS

● Realize your memory's true potential by training it to perform quickly and efficiently.

● Make positive memories for babies by ensuring their environment is rich and stimulating.

> 66 A great and beautiful invention is memory, always useful both for learning and for life. 99
>
> *Dialexeis*, 400 BC

▼ **Learning language skills**
Memory plays a crucial role in language development. Infants learn by imitation and practice, storing words in their memory long before they begin to use them in speech.

REMEMBERING AS A CHILD

Exactly when memory starts is a matter of conjecture, but babies are known to recognize voices they heard while they were in the womb, and are said to recognize pieces of music that were played repeatedly before they were born. In their first months, babies begin to recognize the people most often with them, and their surroundings. From the age of one, they develop language skills: while much of this learning is by repetition, toddlers quickly learn to devise their own words or to change existing ones. For example, he or she may say "breaked" instead of "broken," applying a rule memorized subconsciously.

Newborn recognizes voices heard in the womb

Newborn

In the first year, begins to understand familiar words

First year

In second year, starts to learn words by repetition

Second year

From third year, begins to form own words

Third year

MEMORY AND AGING

Memory performance does not deteriorate with age. The blood flow to and oxygen consumption in the brain—two factors that determine its performance—are exactly the same in a healthy 70-year-old and a healthy 20-year-old. Their memories perform equally well. The only area in which overall performance differs is speed of learning. When the older person is given a piece of new information to learn, he or she takes longer than the younger person to absorb it.

▼ **Learning at any age**
While speed of learning may decline with age, retention and recall of information remain as good as ever.

Learns more quickly than 70-year-old

Reads new information

Reads new information

Remembers as well as the 20-year-old

20-year-old

70-year-old

Fact File

As they get older, many people put the worsening performance of their memory down to losing brain cells. However, while we do lose brain cells as we age, it is not at the rate that most people believe. In fact, a 70-year-old person still has about 97 percent of the number of brain cells that he or she had at the age of 25.

WHY MEMORY FAILS

Memory can fail temporarily because of stress or tiredness, both of which affect concentration. Amnesia—partial or complete failure on a long-term basis—may be caused by psychological trauma or by damage to the brain resulting from a blow to the head or conditions such as a tumor, stroke, or swelling of the brain. Amnesia may manifest itself as a difficulty remembering ongoing events, events prior to an incident, or events from childhood. Usually the memory slowly or suddenly comes back, although the memory of the trauma may remain incomplete.

MEMORY AND IQ

A person's IQ is often believed to be fixed, but improving memory skills can increase it. IQ tests examine many areas that are highly developed in people who use memory-training techniques. Three such areas are the power of association—which is a key principle of memory training; spatial awareness—which is enhanced by image creation; and numbers—the recall of numbers is easily improved with memory techniques.

At a Glance

● Memory can operate at an advanced age as well as, if not better than, in youth.

● Memory can be temporarily damaged by stress, tiredness, or psychological trauma.

● An individual's IQ can be raised by improving memory, because the tests examine areas that can be developed by memory skills.

Combining ▶ crucial skills
Try to develop all the main areas of mental performance. Blending them has a synergistic effect—using them all at once is more effective than the sum of using them individually.

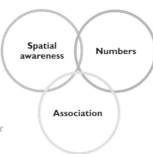

Spatial awareness

Numbers

Association

66 We are what we repeatedly do. Excellence, then, is not an act, but a habit. **99**

Aristotle

IQ TESTS

Tests to assess a person's IQ (intelligence quotient) were first brought into use in the 19th century. They measure your performance in certain mental abilities, and the results are taken as an indication of how you would perform in unmeasured areas. The tests have caused much controversy about whether IQ is a matter of genetics or environment. However, it has been shown that education and environment can affect your score. Memory-training techniques will certainly improve your IQ—by broadening your vocabulary, for example. Another way to increase your score is to practice doing the test: each time you do an IQ test, you learn from the questions asked, so your memory builds up a bank of experience that it can call upon in the future.

Rubik's Cube
A key part of IQ tests measures spatial awareness—our ability to look at things three-dimensionally. Restoring a scrambled Rubik's Cube to its original configuration can enhance this skill.

How Memory Works

The brain is a highly complex human faculty, much of it not yet fully understood. What we do know is that the strength of the connections between the brain's cells, or neurons, is crucial to the performance of the memory.

STRUCTURE OF THE BRAIN

The brain weighs approximately 3 lb (1.3 kg) and has the texture of a hard-boiled egg. The lower part, or cerebellum, controls movement; the midbrain, including the thalamus and hypothalamus, relays sensory information and regulates body systems; and the higher region of the brain, or cerebrum, controls complex functions, including memory. Neurons are the basic unit of the nervous system, conducting impulses around the body. In the brain, they are responsible for, among other things, creating and storing memories. The cerebral cortex—the ridged and folded outer layer of the cerebrum—has the largest concentration of neurons.

FOCUS POINTS

● Harness the power of your brain—it has phenomenal potential, and there is no limit to its capability.

● Learn how to use all the areas of your brain—they work together to form nature's most amazing computer.

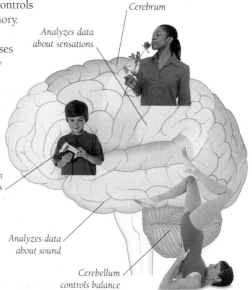

Cerebrum

Analyzes data about sensations

Deals with thought processes

Analyzes data about sound

Cerebellum controls balance

The human brain ▶
The upper and largest part of the brain, the cerebrum, processes complex information. Its different areas have specific functions. Your memory uses several parts of the brain, which can be developed by memory-training techniques.

HOW BRAIN CELLS WORK

The brain has 10 billion cells, or neurons. Each neuron consists of a cell body with radiating branches. These branches consist of one axon and up to 10,000 other projections, called dendrites. The connections between axons and dendrites, which are actually gaps, are known as synapses. Neurotransmitters are chemicals that convey nerve signals across these junctions.

▼ **Structure of a brain cell**
These three brain cells are shown in simplified form. Each has a central nucleus and many branches, each of which has numerous connection points.

Dendrite receives impulses and conducts them to the cell body

Synapse

Nucleus

Axon carries impulses from cell body to other cells

Neuron cell body

Fact File

Your brain is like a vast telephone exchange, shuttling messages between its billions of cells. Imagine that everyone in the world is talking on the telephone at the same time, and that each person is speaking to 10,000 other people. This is the connectivity power of the neurons in the brain. Some scientists claim that the number of connections is greater than the number of atoms in the universe.

CREATING MEMORY TRACES

The electrochemical system of passing signals around the brain allows us to create memories at incredible speed. Each memory has a unique pattern, called a trace, which is formed from connections between neurons. The strength of the trace determines the strength of the memory. You can use memory-training techniques to create more connections and thus strengthen the trace. Signals are constantly passed between the synapses in the brain, forming a virtually infinite network of links. It is the complexity and limitless variety of this network that make the human brain and the memory so powerful.

RECEIVING SENSORY INFORMATION

Sensory memory consists of pieces of information received from our senses—a smell, sound, sight, touch, or taste. Information from each sense is sent to different parts of the brain. Each piece of information is stored for a maximum of one-tenth of a second, until the next piece is received. When the pieces of sensory information arrive in quick succession, the brain registers a continuous sensation. Sensory information is examined and filtered, and is converted to a memory only if it is of particular significance.

▲ **Evoking the past**
A single smell—a particular perfume, for instance—is often enough to trigger a flood of memories decades after an event.

Fact File

Momentous events can instantly create long-term memories. For example, many people vividly remember where they were when they heard the news of John F. Kennedy's assassination, Princess Diana's death, or the attack on the World Trade Center on September 11, 2001.

REMEMBERING IN THE SHORT TERM

Short-term memory is also known as the working memory. It holds information for between ten and 20 seconds and usually retains no more than about seven pieces of information at once. When you are reading a sentence, your short-term memory stores the beginning of the sentence while you are reading the rest of it, so that you can comprehend the whole.

EXPLAINING DEJA VU

Deja vu is a phenomenon that may give us a clue about how memory works (and what happens when it goes wrong). The term means "already seen" in French, and describes an overwhelming sense of familiarity with a situation that a person has never, to their knowledge, experienced before. As many as 70 percent of people report having experienced deja vu. It has been ascribed to a mismatching of signals in the brain, which causes it to mistake the present for the past. Some psychoanalysts believe deja vu is related to a past-life experience; others attribute it to fantasy or wish fulfillment.

Experiencing deja vu
With deja vu, a location can seem as familiar as a place visited on vacation, but that sense of familiarity—unlike photographs—fades in seconds.

REMEMBERING IN THE LONG TERM

Information that has been well consolidated is stored in the long-term memory. If you are to improve learning, it is your long-term memory that you must develop. There are two main types of long-term memory—implicit and explicit. Implicit memory is concerned with learning new skills, such as riding a bike or swimming: once learned, these skills are rarely forgotten. Explicit memory is concerned with recollecting data and facts learned throughout your life to date.

FOCUS POINTS

● Note how the memory uses signals received from the five senses to make judgments and decisions.

● Learn how to commit information from the working memory to the long-term memory.

MAKING MEMORY LONG-TERM

How well you recall things depends on the strength of the trace created in your brain at the time of learning. If something lodged in the short-term memory is very powerful—for example, the birth of a child—it can instantly become an unforgettable, long-term memory. You can train your brain to encode information so it creates a strong trace and is then easily and quickly recalled at any time. An experience that is repeated and associated with other memories can become a long-term memory.

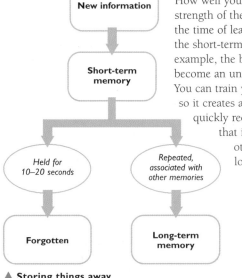

New information

↓

Short-term memory

↓

Held for 10–20 seconds

Repeated, associated with other memories

↓

Forgotten

Long-term memory

▲ Storing things away
You can move a new piece of information into your long-term memory by rehearsing it, or by linking it with other things already in the memory.

Practices new skill

Learning a new skill ▶
Once a skill such as juggling has been lodged in the long-term memory, it can be recalled at any future time.

Why Improve Your Memory?

*E*mbarking on memory training without having an objective is like going on a journey without a destination. Identify the areas in your life where you would benefit from a more powerful memory. Focusing on them will give you the incentive to learn.

REALIZING YOUR MEMORY'S POTENTIAL

Your memory can be trained, just like any other human faculty. With the correct techniques, you can teach your memory to do anything you choose. You can improve it by training and practice in exactly the same way as you do when you learn to play a musical instrument or to speak a foreign language. Memory-training techniques work—simply because they develop the natural ability of your brain.

▲ **Learning through practice**
Practicing memory-training techniques will improve your performance, as with any other skill—such as piano playing.

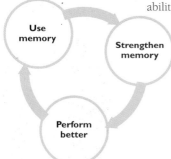

Use memory

Strengthen memory

Perform better

▲ **Creating a positive cycle**
Using your memory makes it stronger; once you have confidence in your memory, you use it more.

BOOSTING CONFIDENCE

A lack of confidence in your memory paralyzes it and locks information inside it. With training, you will become confident in your ability to recall information quickly and accurately. The improvement is self-generating: the more you use your memory in the correct way, the better it performs; the better memory performs, the more you use it. You will then notice not only your confidence but also your social skills improving, as you find yourself accurately and easily remembering people's names and the details of their lives.

At a Glance

- Confidence in your memory will improve your social skills.
- Exam performance can be improved by memory training.
- Remembering the names and details of colleagues helps to build rapport.

IMPROVING STUDY SKILLS

Memory training cannot help you to understand new information better, but it will enable you to store it and recall it correctly. This improves your chances of recalling information quickly and accurately in an exam. So you will actually enjoy testing your skills in the exam, as well as studying for it, rather than finding it tedious and painful— and you will be rewarded with a better result.

PERFORMING MORE EFFICIENTLY AT WORK

Improving your memory increases your efficiency at work. For example, you will spend less time looking up facts and checking appointments. Having complete and accurate information at your fingertips speeds up problem-solving and decision-making, and remembering the names of colleagues, clients, and customers makes for better working and customer relationships.

▼ **Keeping up to date at work**
A manager points out to an employee her need to master a new technique. Her success or failure depends on her willingness to improve her memory.

Manager notices overall improvement and promotes employee to team leader

Employee practices memory skills, masters new program—and also improves personal skills

Manager tells employee she is letting her team down by not learning a new computer program

Employee fails to master new skill, and is moved off the team

Assessing Your Memory

What is your attitude to your memory? Respond to the following statements by marking the answers closest to your experience. Be as honest as you can: if your answer is "Never," mark Option 1; if it is "Always," mark Option 4; and so on. Add up your scores, and refer to the analysis to see how you feel.

Options

1. Never
2. Occasionally
3. Frequently
4. Always

How Do You Respond?

	1	2	3	4
1 I do not believe memory can be trained.	☑	☐	☐	☐
2 I feel my memory is getting worse as I age.	☐	☑	☐	☐
3 My short-term memory lets me down.	☐	☐	☑	☐
4 My long-term memory is erratic.	☐	☑	☐	☐
5 I have difficulty recalling names.	☐	☐	☐	☑
6 My memory fails me in exams.	☐	☑	☐	☐
7 I find learning dull and boring.	☐	☑	☐	☐
8 I have no confidence in my memory.	☐	☑	☐	☐
9 My diet is left to chance.	☑	☐	☐	☐

	1	2	3	4
10 I do little or no physical exercise.	☑	☐	☐	☐
11 My lifestyle is stressful.	☐	☑	☐	☐
12 My sleep quality varies.	☐	☐	☑	☐
13 I have a negative outlook.	☑	☐	☐	☐
14 I believe I have no imagination.	☐	☑	☐	☐
15 I have no motivation to improve myself.	☑	☐	☐	☐
16 I fail to meet targets.	☐	☑	☐	☐
17 I find it hard to concentrate.	☐	☐	☑	☐
18 I make no special effort to memorize.	☐	☑	☐	☐

	1	2	3	4		1	2	3	4
19 I am lacking in confidence.	☑	☐	☐	☐	**26** I rely on a calculator for arithmetic.	☑	☐	☐	☐
20 I feel I am not in control of my life.	☐	☑	☐	☐	**27** When making a speech, I use notes.	☐	☐	☑	☐
21 I find some words hard to remember.	☐	☑	☐	☐	**28** Learning a foreign language is daunting.	☐	☐	☐	☑
22 I get to the store and forget what I came for.	☐	☑	☐	☐	**29** I leave it to chance that I will recall facts.	☐	☑	☐	☐
23 Remembering times and dates is difficult.	☐	☑	☐	☐	**30** Mental exercises are pointless.	☑	☐	☐	☐
24 I have trouble memorizing new PINs.	☐	☑	☐	☐	**31** I am skeptical about memory techniques.	☐	☑	☐	☐
25 I use a paper or electronic organizer.	☐	☑	☐	☐	**32** I do not believe I can improve my memory.	☑	☐	☐	☐

Analysis

When you have added up your scores, look at the analysis below to see how you feel about your attitude to your memory and its performance. Then note the areas where you perform best or worst, and work particularly on your weak areas.

32–64 You have a healthy attitude, and your memory performs very well. Build on that and it will be even more effective.

65–95 Your attitude and performance are good overall. But you could do better if you improved your skills.

96–128 Your attitude to your memory and the factors that affect it is poor. Take the necessary steps to improve your performance in all areas of life.

My weakest areas are:

short term memory
and speed of memorization

My strongest areas are:

very smart and
hardworking.

Developing Your Memory Potential

To develop the power of your memory, you must focus on overall physical well-being and on the mental attitudes that will contribute to its success.

Supporting Your Memory

The memory does not work in isolation, but as a part of the brain and the body as a whole. It follows that, if you are to maximize your memory's potential, you must adopt a range of simple support measures to keep your body in good working order.

LAYING THE FOUNDATIONS

Most people assume that their memories will work at all times, under all conditions, with unerring accuracy, and at great speed. In reality, this laissez-faire attitude results in inconsistent memory performance. Like other parts of your body, your memory needs to be nurtured on a constant and long-term basis if it is to perform at its full potential. The first step to building a solid foundation for memory-training techniques is simply to appreciate how important it is to make a conscious effort to keep your mind in good working order.

▲ **Keeping fit in mind and body**
For peak performance, your memory— like your body—requires an approach that puts high value on a healthy and invigorating lifestyle.

EATING WELL

The power of food as a booster for good memory performance should not be underestimated. It is vital that neurotransmitters, which control your ability to pass information between nerve cells, are maintained well. Because the brain is susceptible to oxidation, antioxidants are important. These include foods that are rich in vitamin C, vitamin E, carotenoids, and selenium. Other brain boosters are fatty acids, especially Omega-3 fatty acids; B vitamins; and certain minerals. To maximize your intake of these nutrients, eat as much fresh food as you can and cook it as little as possible. *Ginkgo biloba*, taken as a supplement, is believed to improve the flow of blood to the brain.

▲ **Sustaining the brain**
Oily fish, including salmon, and broccoli, rich in antioxidants, are some of the foods important for mental performance.

Natural Brain and Memory Enhancers

Nutrient	Source
Antioxidants: **vitamin C, vitamin E,** **selenium, carotenoids**	Citrus fruits, broccoli, peppers, carrots, sweet potato, kale, spinach, seafood, grains, brazil nuts, soybeans, vegetable oils
Omega-3 fatty acids	Oily fish (sardines, salmon, mackerel, tuna, herring, anchovies), olive oil
B vitamins: **B1, B3, B6, B12**	Poultry, fish, milk, cereal, nuts, wholegrains, beans, leafy green vegetables
Minerals: **boron, magnesium,** **zinc**	Apples, pears, beans, peas, whole wheat, nuts, dark turkey meat, shellfish
Ginkgo biloba	Herbal extract, widely available as a supplement

EXERCISING YOUR BODY AND MIND

Your physical health plays an important role in your mental performance. Your brain uses 20 percent of your oxygen intake, although it makes up only three percent of your total bodyweight. Improved blood flow as a result of a cardiovascular training provides essential oxygen and so has a direct impact on your brain's performance. Exercise should be done at moderate intensity— that is, you should never be more than slightly out of breath. Aim for a minimum of 20 minutes, three times a week.

▲ **Exercising for a healthy mind**
Exercise increases blood flow around the body, thus raising the amount of oxygen available. This allows the brain to function better. Exercise should be pleasurable, so choose something you enjoy—and notice how it makes you feel more alert.

Practices relaxation exercises

Meditates for a few minutes each day

▲ **Taking time out**
Your memory will not perform at its best if you are stressed or have too much on your mind. Take time out each day to unwind physically and mentally.

REDUCING THE STRESS FACTOR

Training your memory will improve both your efficiency and your capability, but it is still important not to have too much to cope with. Avoid trying to juggle too many tasks at once. Learn time-management techniques so you can maintain order in your life and feel in control. If you naturally tend to take on too much, learn to say no to people. Use stress-reduction techniques, such as simple relaxation exercises or meditation, to alleviate the pressure on you at home and work. Make sure you have a little time just for yourself every day, when you retreat from the world and do something you enjoy. Plan to spend dedicated, relaxed time with your family and friends every day, and make sure that you take regular vacations.

BEING AWARE OF BIORHYTHMS

Everyone has a biorhythm, a fluctuation in their system that leads to performance peaks and troughs. This rhythm affects your memory: many people find their memory is at its best in the early morning and mid-evening. Because energy levels are linked to temperature, you can check your biorhythm, and hence your memory performance, by monitoring your temperature—high temperature levels usually reflect high energy levels. Make three-hourly temperature checks throughout the day and plot the results on a chart. Do this for a week and note when your optimum time usually occurs.

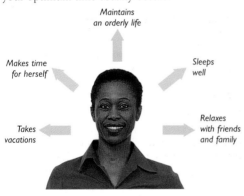

Maintains
an orderly life

Makes time
for herself

Sleeps
well

Takes
vacations

Relaxes
with friends
and family

FOCUS POINTS

● Take regular exercise in order to increase your attention level, which will in itself boost your memory function.

● Take steps to ensure you regularly get a good night's sleep—without it, it is difficult to concentrate or learn new tasks.

◀ **Creating a good regimen**
A way of life that promotes general health and well-being is a way of life that will also keep your memory in good shape. In addition to eating well and exercising regularly, eliminate stress and make time for relaxation.

SLEEPING WELL

Sleep is vital for good health in general, and lack of sleep can contribute to mental confusion. It is also believed that sleep plays an important role in the consolidation of memory. The same areas that are involved in learning new tasks in our waking hours continue to process information while we are asleep. So sleep allows our brains to store new information in the memory for future use. It follows that sleeping well is important for good memory.

Useful Exercises

▶ Give your brain a quick boost by jogging in place for a few minutes.

▶ Do stretching exercises. Apart from helping you to keep joints supple, this will motivate you to exercise regularly.

▶ When you practice breathing exercises for relaxation, concentrate on making each breath in and each breath out deeper, longer, and slower than the last one.

Thinking Constructively

*B*efore you start work on your memory skills, first consider how positive you are when faced with a challenge. Then focus on your own particular way of thinking. A positive mental attitude can make all the difference.

66 Minds are like parachutes; they work better when open. 99

Thomas Dewar

▼ **Developing your potential**
Like training for a sport, memory training may at first have setbacks, but with a positive approach, you will win through.

HAVING A POSITIVE OUTLOOK

Your attitude to life determines your quality of life. If you have a negative approach, you view everything as an obstacle, and think of excuses to stay where you are. If you have a positive attitude, you view everything as a challenge to be relished and will enjoy the end result, whatever it is. You will face challenges as you practice memory-improving techniques, but a positive mental attitude ensures that you do not fall at the first hurdle. So do not blame your bad memory for everything, and discard any misconceptions you may have that areas of memory that already perform well cannot be developed. This allows you to feel positive about your memory and more likely to rely on it, so improving it further.

▼ **Thinking the best of yourself**
A positive outlook on life will give you the faith that you can develop your memory to its full potential.

Feel positive about memory training → Believe you can improve memory → Improve your memory

THINKING ABOUT THINKING

Thinking is something that most people do automatically, without contemplating exactly how they are going about it. This usually means that individuals think in one particular way most of the time. Your thinking patterns mold your thoughts, perceptions, attitudes, and, ultimately, your actions and behavior. When people talk about opening up the mind, they tend to mean thinking about something in a different way from usual. No one style of thinking is better than another, but to maximize your memory potential you need to learn to think in ways that mirror those in which the brain functions naturally. The recommended memory-training techniques follow this principle—and all thinking skills can be easily learned.

Self-Talk

The words you say to yourself are crucial to your feeling good and achieving success. To put yourself in a positive frame of mind, repeat the following statements to yourself:

66 *My memory can perform fantastic feats.* 99

66 *Today I am going to have a wonderful day.* 99

66 *I can achieve anything I want to, as long as I put my mind to it.* 99

66 *I will view any obstacles as challenges to be overcome.* 99

Reorganizing a List

Make a list

Sort by initial letter

Sort by type

Sort by color

Go shopping!

THINKING CREATIVELY

One key step to realizing your memory's potential is recognizing that by nature our brains work with images. You have a virtually infinite capacity for creating images: you can imagine anything you want—even things you have never seen, if they are described in detail. By associating something with a strong image of an item you already know, you dramatically improve the memory's ability to learn, retain, and recall it. Also fundamental to memory training is the brain's natural propensity to organize information in patterns. Look for patterns and, if order is not paramount, reorganize the information. For example, when you have a list, look for words beginning with the same letter. See if things fit into categories: perhaps five things are items of stationery and four are household objects. Are any of the things the same color? By breaking a large group of things into several smaller ones, you make it easier to assimilate.

23

Devising an Action Plan

Setting goals not only motivates you into action, it also focuses your mind, and maximizes your energy to achieve the level of performance you set yourself. In addition, goal-setting minimizes time wastage, and prevents inconsistency of results.

Focuses the mind by setting an end time

DEFINING YOUR GOAL

SMART is a well-known acronym for setting objectives. Be **S**pecific about what you are trying to do. Say, for example, you are studying German; your goal might be learning a total of 2,000 words. This a very specific goal. **M**easure your performance as you go along: group the words and test yourself often. Make sure your goal is always **A**chievable, and alter it if it turns out to be too easy or too difficult: there is no point in setting yourself up to fail. Your goal must also be **R**elevant: increasing your vocabulary will improve your use of the language. Finally, set a **T**ime by which you will have learned your 2,000 words.

▲ **Setting the target**
Clear parameters act as a spur to achieving objectives. Fix a time—or set an alarm—for completing each goal.

Useful Exercises

▶ Write your goals on a whiteboard in the spare bedroom or garage, as well as in your planner.

▶ Stick pictures of your holiday destination by your written goals as an incentive to learn the language.

▶ Practice setting goals with others, so you can help each other achieve them.

TIMETABLING YOUR GOALS

Goals can be small or big, short-term or long-term. Break bigger goals down into mini-goals. For example, if your overall goal is learning 2,000 German words in five months, you could break it down by setting a goal of 400 words a month, 100 words a week, and 14 words a day. Your target might be to learn those 14 words and review the previous ones in an hour. This is a relevant and achievable goal, set within a time-restricted framework. Keep a log of how you are achieving your goals, and recalibrate if need be.

The SMART Formula

Key	Goal
Specific	Be specific about the type of goal you are setting.
Measurable	Choose a goal that you can measure.
Achievable	Alter your goal if necessary so it remains achievable.
Relevant	Make sure your goal is something you can identify with.
Time	Set a fixed period of time within which to complete your goal.

GETTING STARTED

Memory-training techniques, no matter how potentially successful, are of no use at all unless you put them into action. An action plan is a dedicated way to help you get the most out of the training techniques. It will stop you from procrastinating. Because you can see clearly the actions that you need to take, you will be more likely to do them. You will enjoy the many benefits that improved learning brings. Your mind will be focused on developing and improving yourself. And the pleasure of making big strides forward will benefit your whole life.

▼ **Writing out an action plan**
Write your goals down, with times, and review them daily. This pushes the brain subconsciously to make them a reality.

Start time and finish time for each task clearly defined

Specific goal, limited in scope, set for each day

Monday April 7	7 pm–8 pm	Learn how brain and memory works
Saturday April 12	3 pm–4 pm	Read up on memory-training techniques
Wednesday April 16	8 pm–9 pm	Choose one technique and try it out

Separate, short-term goals make up bigger long-term goal

Goal of improving memory broken down into mini-goals

Making Techniques Work for You

The key to being able to do something well is to have confidence in your ability to do it. Mastering memory techniques will boost your self-confidence. Belief in yourself can be the difference between success and failure.

66 It is not enough to have a good mind. The main thing is to use it well. 99

Descartes

MAINTAINING SELF-BELIEF

Confidence in your memory comes from practice and application of the training techniques, and also from knowing that the techniques are all extremely well founded. They are used by millions of people worldwide in their day-to-day lives. There is no mystique to the process: memory record holders and world champions use exactly the same techniques as you will use.

◀ **Becoming adept**
Mastering the techniques that are practiced by memory world champions will give you the confidence to apply them whenever you need to memorize anything—for example, when playing cards.

Things to Do	Things to Avoid
✔ Do be adventurous and try adapting the techniques for yourself. Anything can be memorized.	✘ Avoid trying to do too much at once. Pick out one specific task to focus on, and learn from that.
✔ Do make notes on how you approach each memorizing task. At a later date you can refer back to them and learn from that experience.	✘ Avoid using the techniques at inappropriate times. Use them at home before applying them to your work.
✔ Do share your experiences with others. It will encourage them to improve their memory, too.	✘ Avoid long, irregular practice sessions. Practice little and often—15 minutes a day is more effective than two long sessions per week.

PROGRAMMING PRACTICE TIME

Learning to improve your memory through training is the same as learning any other skill, physical or mental: you need plenty of practice if the techniques are going to work successfully. A steady but continuous program of personal development will help you improve. Find things to memorize, such as a list of names, and practice doing so, perhaps when out walking, or sitting on a bus or train.

▲ **Following a program**
Plan and stick to a program for practicing memory techniques. Make use of the time you spend traveling on public transportation, for example—tune out distractions, and practice memorizing a list of names, perhaps, or a telephone number.

▼ **Developing your skills**
Start by learning the techniques, then practice them thoroughly. Only then can you use them to their full potential.

Learn the techniques	→	Practice the techniques	→	Use the techniques

ADAPTING THE TEMPLATES

The techniques are only the first stage in the process of improving your memory. The key to success is learning to apply the various techniques to your own circumstances and experiences. Think of them as a mental toolbox: as you develop your skills, you will pick the most suitable one for your needs. Your ability to adapt the techniques will increase as you practice the generic exercises. It is like learning to drive: one person may want to drive a cab, another a racecar, but both have to pass their driving test before adapting their skills to their specific requirements.

FOCUS POINTS

● Practice memory skills in the same way as any other endeavor—with application and dedication.

● Modify the techniques to suit your own personal needs. You can use them however you choose, as long as they help recall.

Training Your Memory

The way to improve your memory is to learn specific techniques. Build on this foundation, and you will be able to take your memory performance to any level you choose.

Introducing the Principles

Memory-training techniques make the most of the way the memory works naturally. The techniques covered here offer different ways of ordering information. You can use them alone or in combination, according to what is being learned.

> **FOCUS POINT**
>
> ● Develop a solid bedrock of memory-training techniques—all future skills will be built on this.

▲ **Making visual patterns**
Look at these two sets of dots. There are 16 dots in each set. The dots on the left are randomly ordered, while those on the right are arranged as four rows of four. By rearranging the dots into a logical pattern, you make it much easier for the brain to deal with them.

ORGANIZING INFORMATION

For maximum efficiency and minimum loss of information, it is vital to organize the information you receive. Breaking down or arranging the information into a simple pattern is an easy first step toward organizing it. Put simply, if your brain takes an active part in processing the information in some way, it is more likely to remember it accurately. Ways to encourage your brain to engage actively with information include concentrating harder and using your visual and other senses to reorganize the data into a more memorable format.

IMPROVING CONCENTRATION

Concentration is an essential habit to develop when you are using any memory technique. Compare your recollection of a television show you watched while doing something else at the same time with your recall of a show on which you concentrated fully. In the first case, it is likely to be less accurate and detailed than in the second. Teach yourself to concentrate more by imagining that you will be asked questions later. Try this out: listen to the radio and then answer questions set by a friend. This process of reviewing information after initial learning is also vital to improving memory.

At a Glance

- Organization is as essential to your memory as it is to running an office.

- Organization in itself increases memory retention.

- We all have the ability to concentrate well.

- Your senses can be trained to notice more detail.

- A multisensory approach to learning is effective in improving memory.

Concentrates solely on book

◀ **Being focused**
Complete concentration is necessary for total recall. When you are reading and want to memorize the material, you cannot, for example, listen to the radio as well.

Radio turned off

FOCUS POINT

- To heighten all your senses, imagine what something smells, tastes, and feels like, as well as how it sounds and looks.

USING YOUR SENSES

Sight and hearing are the senses most used in learning. Develop your seeing and hearing so that they become more acute. Artists "see" 30 percent more than the average person because they are used to looking at things in more detail and from a different perspective. To improve your senses, make a conscious effort to notice detail. Spend one day observing the color of people's eyes, for example, and the next what type of nose or ears they have. Listen carefully to their voices— do they have an accent or a favorite phrase?

USING LOCATIONS

Think about how you sometimes mentally retrace your steps when you have lost something and are trying to remember where you last had it. This is something your brain does naturally, and is the key to an important memory-training technique. The "journey" technique uses a route through a series of familiar locations, such as rooms in your house or office, and places into each location a mental image of one of the pieces of information. This allows you to recall in a particular order.

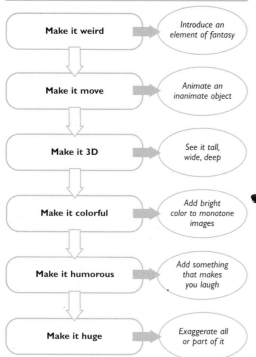

Image Creation Principles

Make it weird	*Introduce an element of fantasy*
Make it move	*Animate an inanimate object*
Make it 3D	*See it tall, wide, deep*
Make it colorful	*Add bright color to monotone images*
Make it humorous	*Add something that makes you laugh*
Make it huge	*Exaggerate all or part of it*

CREATING IMAGES

The foundation on which all memory-skills training is based is creating mental images from the information that you are learning. The most memorable images are the ones that are completely out of the ordinary. Use Image Creation Principles to embellish the image, making it unique and unforgettable. As your eye for detail improves, you will find it becomes easier to make your images vivid.

▲ **Creating wacky images**
Here, "beach ball" is made more memorable by turning it into something that has movement, fantasy, and humor.

▲ Practicing association skills
Play association games—perhaps on car journeys: ask your companions what is the first thing they think of when you give them a word. This speeds up the process of making associations, a technique that helps to improve memory.

USING ASSOCIATIONS

Your brain loves to form links between pieces of information, building up a repertoire of associations. When your brain receives new information, it searches in your long-term memory for something the same or similar so that it can "understand" what it is. This happens in an instant and is not a conscious process. Creating associations is very helpful in improving memory. By actively creating a personal link for your brain to hook on to, you give your memory something to work with, helping it to retrieve it later.

STORING INFORMATION

Organization is the key to successful management of information in many areas of life. Libraries are a good example: without a sorting and encoding system to organize the books, a library could not function at all. Most offices have an efficient filing system whereby any information that may be needed at a later date is put in a folder, which is placed in a filing cabinet. Memory techniques do the same for your mind whenever you receive new pieces of information. They create a framework—patterns, for instance, or locations—into which you place information for future recollection. This will give your memory the chance to process and store information in the way that will facilitate the most efficient recall.

Places papers needed for future reference into folders

▲ Filing information
Just like a filing cabinet, your memory works most efficiently when information is sorted and stored in a logical way.

Remembering Names

Many people struggle to remember names. They try all kinds of memory aids, with varying degrees of success, but using a technique that is specifically for learning names eliminates the need for anything else and gives you total confidence.

Looks at photographs of a family wedding and is reminded of a childhood vacation

▲ **Bringing back memories**
Memory works by association, so a photograph of one event often brings another occasion to mind. The same principle of association can be used to memorize and recall names.

USING THE ASSOCIATION TECHNIQUE

When you remember someone's name after having met them only once, you make them feel special. In a business situation, when you are working with clients or customers, it is an advantage to be able to call them by their name. In the first crucial minutes of meeting someone new, using their name can help create a rapport between you. There is a simple way to improve your memory for names: the key is to tap into your imagination. The technique for remembering names long-term is known as the Association Technique. It involves two steps: creating an image and attaching it to a person.

Useful Exercises

▶ Pick out names from the newspaper each day or find a book of babies' names. Practice creating images for each one.

▶ Begin by applying the name techniques to individuals you already know, then proceed to new people.

▶ Explain the techniques to other people. Apart from helping you consolidate them, this is fun, and a great icebreaker in a social situation.

CREATING AN IMAGE FROM A PERSON'S NAME

When you first hear a person's name, immediately create an image in association with it. Learn to listen to and use the associations that come into your brain first—these are the ones your memory will find easiest to recall. For example, the name Julie might prompt an image of jewelry because the words sound similar, while Bill might make you think of a dollar bill. The surname Booth might bring up the picture of a telephone booth, or Singh might make you think of a microphone used for singing. Observe the person's face to fix it in your mind, looking for distinctive features.

At a Glance

● Being able to remember names helps you professionally as well as socially.

● The first thing that comes into your head is often the most memorable association.

● When you first meet someone, it helps if you notice something distinctive.

● The Association Technique can be used together with Image Creation Principles.

Listen to name	→	Create image	→	Attach image

▲ **Using association**
Train yourself to let an image come into your head when you first hear someone's name. Then create a link in your mind between the image and the person whose name you are memorizing.

ATTACHING THE IMAGE

After you have met the person, use the Image Creation Principles to elaborate the image you have created for the name, then attach it to the person. For Julie, your image was jewelry—you might see her wearing a mass of jewels. Make the image stronger by imagining them shining brightly, hurting your eyes. Hear the chink of her gold chains as she walks. When you meet the person again, seeing their face prompts you to recall the image and that triggers their name.

Notices unusual shirt and uses this as his image

Mentally exaggerates the shirt to make it more memorable

◀ **Looking for a link**
When you first meet someone, notice anything distinctive—for example, a colorful shirt—and link it to their name.

USING THE SLUG TECHNIQUE

A second system to help memorize names is known by the acronym SLUG. The letters stand for **S**low down the introduction, **L**isten to the name, **U**se the name, **G**o over the name. When you are first introduced to someone (this is when the new name is most easily lost) there is usually very little time to implement the Association Technique effectively. The SLUG Technique is a simple, four-stage process that gives you a chance to capture the name and recall it in the short term—when most people forget it.

Listens carefully to name

Uses name in greeting

Slowing the introduction ▶
The more time you take over an introduction, the more likely you are to catch the other person's name in the first place and then to remember it.

Using the SLUG Technique

Action to Take		Reason for Action
Have a brief conversation	**Slow down the introduction**	Improves chances of remembering name
Concentrate hard when name is first given	**Listen to the name**	Name may not be used again after introduction
Use name three times during conversation	**Use the name**	Repetition of name cements it in memory
Review name at end of day and again next day	**Go over the name**	Recall is lost if not reviewed within 48 hours

Case Study

NAME: Li
ISSUE: Embarrassment
OBJECTIVE: To remember names

Li finds she recognizes people, but cannot recall names. She decides to try out memory techniques. When she is introduced to Joe, she looks him in the face and notices a distinguishing feature. She uses his name several times. After they part, she exaggerates that distinctive feature in her mind, and links it with the name Joe. Later, and the next day, she repeats his name. When she meets Joe a year later, she is pleased to find she remembers his name easily.

LISTENING, USING, AND REVIEWING

If you do not listen to the other person's name in the first place, you may find there is no chance of picking it up later on. So make a point of concentrating at the moment their name is given to you, and consciously take it in. Next, it is vital that you actually use the new name. If possible, use it three times during your first meeting—immediately after you are introduced, during your conversation, and when you say goodbye. Even if it is just a brief introduction, you can still acknowledge the person by name. Finally, it is crucial that you remind yourself of the name shortly after you part company, and then again the next day—nearly 80 percent of new information is forgotten within a day or two if it is not reviewed.

66 Forgive your enemies, but never forget their names. 99

John F. Kennedy

COMBINING TECHNIQUES

Both the Association Technique and the SLUG Technique work very well on their own for memorizing names. However, to strengthen the chances of remembering a name when you meet someone new, you can also use both techniques together. Apply the SLUG Technique while you are being introduced to the other person and then, either during or after the conversation, use the Association Technique to link the name to the person. In this way, both the person and their name are stored in your memory and can easily be recalled when you next meet them or need to use their name.

FOCUS POINTS

● Ask a question when you first meet someone, perhaps about the journey. This creates rapport—and slows the introduction.

● Shortly after you have met someone new, make a conscious effort to find an image to which you can attach their name.

Remembering Words and Letters

To remember a group of names or words—as in a list—or a string of letters, use one of two straightforward techniques. Acronyms create a trigger for the memory, while the Phonetic Letter Technique applies images to letters.

FOCUS POINT

● Try to make acronyms as a first step in memorizing lists—most lists can be rearranged to create one.

MAKING ACRONYMS

Acronyms are an age-old method of remembering lists. To create an acronym, take the initial letter of each item and arrange them to make a word. For example, the five Great Lakes are Huron, Michigan, Superior, Ontario, and Erie. Reorder them as Huron, Ontario, Michigan, Erie, Superior, and the initial letters create the acronym HOMES.

▲ **Getting the order right**
To memorize the points of the compass— North, East, South, West—in clockwise order, you might use the acronym Naughty Elephants Squirt Water.

▼ **Making lists manageable**
Use more than one acronym if you have a particularly long list to remember. Break the list down into groups—by color, for example—then create an acronym for each group.

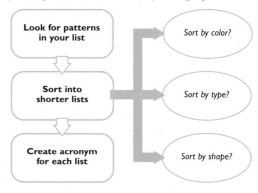

Look for patterns in your list → Sort by color?

Sort into shorter lists → Sort by type?

Create acronym for each list → Sort by shape?

USING EXTENDED ACRONYMS

Extended acronyms take the initial letters of words and use them as the initial letters of words in a sentence. They are useful when you need to recall items in a certain order. For example, a popular acronym for the colors of the rainbow in correct order (Red, Orange, Yellow, Green, Blue, Indigo, Violet) is "Richard Of York Gave Battle In Vain."

USING THE PHONETIC LETTER TECHNIQUE

Single or multiple letters crop up in many places, from passwords to car license plates. Most patterns of letters do not lend themselves to images, so they need to be converted into something that the memory can hook on to. The Phonetic Letter Technique uses the phonetic alphabet, an international system for English-speaking countries that allocates a word to each letter. That word can be used to create an image. The following is the list of words.

A	Alpha	**J**	Juliet	**S**	Sierra		
B	Bravo	**K**	Kilo	**T**	Tango		
C	Charlie	**L**	Lima	**U**	Uniform		
D	Delta	**M**	Mike	**V**	Victor		
E	Echo	**N**	November	**W**	Whiskey		
F	Foxtrot	**O**	Oscar	**X**	X-ray		
G	Golf	**P**	Papa	**Y**	Yankee		
H	Hotel	**Q**	Quebec	**Z**	Zulu		
I	India	**R**	Romeo				

▲ **Remembering passwords**
Letters are difficult to remember, but you can use images—which your memory finds easier to recall—in their place. This is an ideal technique for remembering your computer password, for example.

PERSONALIZING THE IMAGES

The next step is to create images to go with each word. For example, for K–Kilo, your image might be weighing scales (in kilograms), for W–Whiskey, a bottle of whiskey. It is vital to create your own images—images that you will find easy to recall. Recall the image, and that will bring back the word, which will bring back the letter. To remember a string of letters, make up a story using your images in the appropriate order.

◀ **Making the alphabet memorable**
Write down all the letters and words of the phonetic alphabet. Next to each word write or draw an image that you associate with it.

Remembering Lists

The Journey Technique is a highly versatile and phenomenally powerful method of learning lists. It enables you to remember large amounts of information, from a week's planner entries to important historical dates for an exam.

UNDERSTANDING THE TECHNIQUE

This technique is perhaps the oldest known memory aid. It works on the principle of mentally putting information you need to memorize into a familiar location. This gives you somewhere to go to retrieve it when it is needed. Since the technique also employs images and association, it employs all the brain's natural memory tools to maximum effect.

FOCUS POINTS

● Master the Journey Technique and you will be able to memorize a very long list of objects quickly and easily.

● Once you have chosen your journey, write the details down to fix it in your memory.

▼ **Making connections**
This age-old technique enables you to memorize a list by making a mental link between the items on the list and places that your brain already knows.

Make a list of things to remember	→	Design a journey in a familiar location	→	Insert your objects into your journey

Father of the oral tradition
Homer's Odyssey and Iliad were recited from memory and were passed down the generations orally.

ANCIENT GREECE AND ROME

The history of memory skills goes back as far as the days of the ancient Greeks. The word "mnemonic," meaning memory aid, is derived from the name of the Greek goddess of memory, Mnemosyne. Simonides of Ceos, born in the sixth century BC, is regarded as the pioneer of the art of memory training. He devised the "loci technique" of placing pieces of information in locations in order to make it easier to remember them. The Romans continued to develop this technique—the Room Technique was their adaptation of the same system.

DESIGNING YOUR JOURNEY

Assemble the list of items that you are going to learn—for example, six things you need to take on vacation with you: sunscreen, money, sun hat, swimsuit, book, sunglasses. Choose a place you know well, such as your home or workplace, and start to design a journey within it. So that you remember it easily, the route must follow a logical path from start to finish. The number of stages in your journey must match the number of items you have to learn. The vacation list has six items, so the journey needs six stages. Get a pen and paper and practice creating a journey. Once you have decided on a route, place one object into each stage of the journey.

▼ **Plotting the path**
It is important to make your journey a logical one, in a familiar setting—for example, starting in the entrance hall of a house and working through one room into the adjoining one.

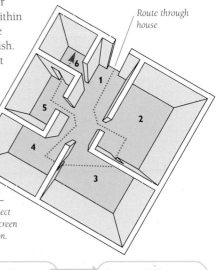

Route through house

▼ **Placing the objects in their locations**
Decide on the locations for each stage of your journey— in this case, six rooms in a house. Then allocate one object to each room. For example, you might visualize the sunscreen in the entrance hall, money in the living room, and so on.

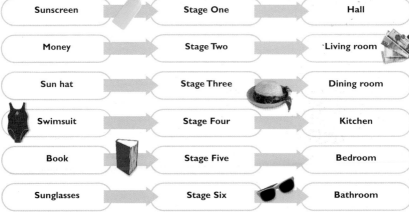

Sunscreen	Stage One	Hall
Money	Stage Two	Living room
Sun hat	Stage Three	Dining room
Swimsuit	Stage Four	Kitchen
Book	Stage Five	Bedroom
Sunglasses	Stage Six	Bathroom

ENVISAGING THE OBJECTS IN THEIR LOCATIONS

Once you have inserted each item on the list into its allocated location on your journey, the next step is to use Image Creation Principles to dream up a ridiculous scenario for each of the rooms. The more wacky the scene, the better the chances of remembering it. The objects on your vacation list do not have a particular order and could have been placed anywhere in the house. Although order is unimportant here, it can sometimes be very important—for example, when you are learning the points to be made in a speech. The chart shows four of the objects on your vacation list, with four imaginary scenarios, in four of the rooms on our sample journey.

▲ **Embellishing the scene**
If your list of things to remember includes sunglasses, for example, you might dream up a scenario in which a kitten sits on the bedroom floor balancing a large, garishly colored pair of sunglasses on its nose.

Imagining the Scene

Stage	Room	Object	Scenario
Stage One	Hall	Sunscreen	You step into the hall, and the floor is covered in sunscreen. You slip on it, fall over, and see your clothes all covered in sunscreen. The empty bottle is laughing at you from the corner.
Stage Two	Living room	Money	You enter the living room and see it is full of bank notes floating in the air. You hear rustling as they flutter into your face. You cannot see your way across the room, the air is so full of them.
Stage Three	Dining room	Sun hat	You go through to the dining room, and the table is covered in sun hats. Some of them are dancing on top of the table. Others are jumping around to a rhythm, as though playing the drums.
Stage Four	Kitchen	Swimsuit	In the kitchen you see swimsuits making themselves a meal. One is looking in the oven, others are chopping vegetables, stirring saucepans, doing the dishes. The swimsuits are chattering to each other as they work.

Things to Do	Things to Avoid
✓ Do trust in the power of your brain.	✗ Avoid spending time creating the "perfect" journey.
✓ Do create your journey quickly.	
✓ Do develop new journeys in new places, such as museums, hotels, or offices.	✗ Avoid using abstract images at first.
	✗ Avoid making your journey too complex until you are confident.
✓ Do expand the technique—once you are proficient—by putting more than one object in each stage.	✗ Avoid spending too much time embellishing your images.

REVIEWING YOUR PROGRESS

Once you have inserted the images into their locations, go through the journey in your mind without looking at what you have written. Have a bit of fun, and go through it backwards. Once you feel happy with it, test yourself by writing the list again on a separate piece of paper. How did you do the second time? You will probably have improved dramatically, both in the number of items you recalled and in the speed with which you recalled them. Your confidence will be greater because you are more sure about the items. The guesswork is now gone—you know that the information you have learned is accurate and complete.

◀ **Testing yourself**
Rehearse your journey until you think you know it. Write your list out as you recall it and then compare it with the original list.

MEMORIZING A NEW LIST

If you are learning a list of information that you are going to need to recall only once or twice, the journey that you create for it can be recycled. Let a month or so elapse after you are finished with it, and then use that journey for a new list. If you are learning a list that you want to keep long-term, however, you will need to think of a new journey especially for that one project. Creating new journeys is not as arduous as it sounds: like any other mental skill, the more you do it, the easier it becomes.

Remembering Numbers

Strings of numbers, from credit card PINs to telephone numbers, are a part of daily life for all of us. The techniques for memorizing numbers are simple to learn— and improving your ability with numbers develops all aspects of mental performance.

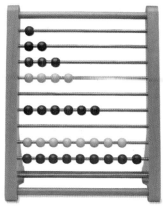

▲ **Working with numbers**
The abacus is an age-old tool for working with numbers, but your most useful tool is your memory. Train it, and you will improve all aspects of your numeracy.

TRYING DIFFERENT SYSTEMS

There are two main systems for helping you memorize numbers: the Number Rhyme and Number Shape System. They are fun and easy to use. Both work on the principle of connecting numbers to images, which you then use to create a story. Try out both systems and see which works better for you. Once you have decided which you prefer, stay with it. Avoid using both methods at the same time or alternating between systems.

Fact File

One of the most remarkable men in the field of memory skills was a Russian called Shereshevsky, known as S. He had synesthesia, a condition in which the senses are blended. His compulsive multisensory approach to learning meant he had a virtually perfect memory. A Russian psychologist, A. R. Luria, tested him in the 1920s and 1930s. However long the series of numbers or words he gave him, S was able to memorize them perfectly, sometimes even 15 years later.

LEARNING THE NUMBER RHYME SYSTEM

The Number Rhyme System works particularly well for auditory thinkers—people who naturally think in terms of sounds and can explain ideas verbally. The first step is to change the numbers 1 to 9 into images that rhyme with the number. One suggested list is given below, but you will remember images more efficiently if you think up your own rhyming words.

0 – Hero	**5** – Beehive
I – Nun	**6** – Sticks
2 – Shoe	**7** – Raven
3 – Tree	**8** – Gate
4 – Door	**9** – Wine

● Train yourself, and there is no limit to how many digits you can recall—most untrained people cannot recall more than seven.

● Learn and apply just ten images and you have mastered the Number Rhyme System—its power lies in its simplicity.

REMEMBERING A SINGLE-DIGIT NUMBER

The next step is to attach the image to the piece of information. There are two different methods: one for single digits, one for multiple digits. To illustrate the single-digit method, imagine a friend has recently moved and you need to memorize his new house number. For example, if the number is 3, to remember this, you might imagine him up a tree—the image chosen here for number 3. Embellish the image by imagining him swinging from branch to branch, eating nuts and berries. To emphasize that it is a house number, you might imagine him building a house in the tree.

REMEMBERING A MULTIPLE-DIGIT NUMBER

The method for memorizing multiple-digit numbers requires you to link the images for each of the numbers by creating a short story. It is vital, of course, to get the images in the correct order. Imagine your burglar alarm code is 4583. You would think up a story involving a door (image for 4), bees in a hive (5), a gate (8), and a tree (3). To help you associate the image with your burglar alarm, you could envisage a burglar with a mask over his face watching the scene.

Converts images back to digits of the phone number

▲ **Memorizing long numbers**
To memorize a telephone number, for example, invent a story using the rhyming words you are using for each digit.

Assessing Your Memory Skills

How well do think you remember series of numbers? Tick any of these statements that describe you accurately.

● I find it difficult to recall statistics accurately. ☐

● I can remember only a handful of historical dates. ☐

● I frequently forget my PIN. ☐

● I do not attempt to learn phone numbers. ☐

● I cannot memorize more than seven digits at once. ☐

Analysis The more items you have checked, the more you need to adopt memory-training techniques to improve your skills. Learn the memory techniques and practice them.

LEARNING THE NUMBER SHAPE SYSTEM

People who are visual thinkers usually find the Number Shape System appropriate. Visual thinkers see pictures in their heads and notice how objects look. The Number Shape System works in a way similar to the Number Rhyme System, but the images you create look similar in shape to the digits, instead of rhyming with them. Here is one suggested list of images.

0 – Baseball
1 – Walking stick
2 – Swan
3 – Handcuffs
4 – Boat sail
5 – Fishhook
6 – Elephant's trunk
7 – Saxophone
8 – Pair of earrings
9 – Balloon

Think about how each image looks like the number, and if you do not find any of them appropriate, choose an image of your own.

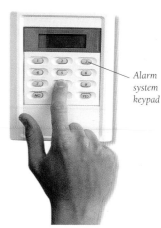

Alarm system keypad

▲ **Using your own images**
An imaginary scenario involving visual images based on the shape of the ten digits is easier for your brain to memorize than a series of numbers—for example, the code for an alarm system.

▲ **Memorizing a multiple-digit number**
Even a short number can be hard to retain with confidence when you are confronted with dozens of other, similar numbers simultaneously—for example, on a flight indicator board at an airport. Use your preferred Number System.

ATTACHING SHAPES TO NUMBERS

Now you must attach your image to the number you are learning. Take the image of each number and link it with the others in a story, in the correct order. For example, you might be meeting someone off Flight Number 267 at the airport. Using the suggested images, you might imagine a swan (2) with an elephant's trunk (6) playing the saxophone (7). To help your memory link the number with a flight, you might make this take place in a plane's cockpit.

MEMORIZING LONG NUMBERS

Many of the numbers you use on a daily basis have more than four digits. The number systems can be further developed to accommodate this by combining your chosen Number System with the Journey Technique. Break down numbers with more than four digits into smaller numbers, then place them in a mini-journey. Break numbers with more than eight digits into at least three sections. Telephone numbers are usually the longest numbers you have to deal with. Imagine that your new doctor's number is (414) 555-1678. Using your chosen Number System, create three stories, one for each part of the number, and place them at the clinic. The journey could be the parking lot, waiting room, and examination room. Your journey must use the images chronologically, so that you recall them in the correct order.

▼ Breaking numbers down
It is much easier to memorize small groups of numbers, so split a five-digit number into a three-digit and a two-digit number; a six-digit number into two three-digit numbers; a seven-digit number into a four-digit number and a three-digit number; and an eight-digit number into two four-digit numbers.

Memorizing Long Numbers

Break number down into smaller units

⬇

Apply Shape or Rhyme System to each unit

⬇

Create a story for each unit

⬇

Think of a journey with the same number of stages

⬇

Place the stories into your journey

Five-digit number

1 2 3 4 5

1 2   3 4 5

Six-digit number

1 2 3 4 5 6

1 2 3   4 5 6

Seven-digit number

1 2 3 4 5 6 7

1 2 3 4   5 6 7

Eight-digit number

1 2 3 4 5 6 7 8

1 2 3 4   5 6 7 8

Using Mind Maps

Mind Mapping is a method of expressing information using color, images, and key words in a structure that radiates from a central core. Its myriad uses include group brainstorming, problem-solving, studying for exams, note-taking, and decision-making.

▲ **Following nature's patterns**
The treelike branches of a Mind Map mirror the natural structure of the brain's neurons.

Beginning to Mind Map ▶
At the hub of a Mind Map is one word or image—for example, a house, representing home. The main branches show the principal areas into which the subject is broken down. Planning content focuses the mind on the subject, allows you to think creatively, and helps recall.

IMPROVING RECALL WITH MIND MAPS

Mind Mapping increases recall significantly during and after the learning process simply because use of color and images together gives the memory more information to hook into than black words printed in linear fashion. The use of key words reduces the amount of information by up to 90 percent, thereby minimizing the amount you are required to remember. The key words trigger other information in the brain. The radiant structure of a Mind Map accurately reflects the structure of the brain and the way we think and learn. The pattern it creates as one large picture allows for excellent memory recall. What is more, making a Mind Map is easy and fun.

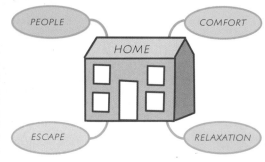

STRUCTURING A MIND MAP

The strength of a Mind Map is in its structure: it gives a snapshot view of the information, and the links and relationships between topics and groups of topics are visually evident. A Mind Map begins with a central image and develops with branches emanating from it. Each branch represents one area to be explored within the main topic. Each main branch has smaller branches radiating from it, and sub-branches may be added, covering further subtopics within that area.

Fact File

The concept of Mind Mapping was first developed in London in the 1970s by Tony Buzan. Mind Maps have since proved highly popular with people of all ages as an effective method of taking notes, a creative way to generate new ideas, and a technique for improving memory and concentration.

FOCUS POINT

● Develop your own Mind Mapping style, always choosing your own words and/or images and colors.

Filling in the detail ▼
Using one color for each of the main branches and its smaller branches helps you think in a organized way.

DRAWING YOUR MIND MAP

Allowing plenty of space, start in the middle of the page and work outward. Draw thick lines for the main branches, each in a different color. Use single key words (rather than a sentence) to represent information, and highlight the main topics by using capital letters. Some people prefer to use pictorial images. Draw lines radiating from each main topic for smaller subjects. Add any detailing you like—perhaps pictures, or an outline for certain words.

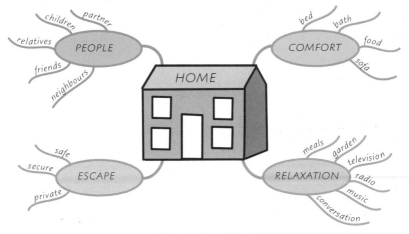

Applying Memory Techniques

There are two stages to mastering memory techniques: learning them and applying them. Familiarize yourself with the range of practical situations in which they can be applied.

Improving Memory Day to Day

The ability to memorize accurately pieces of information that you need on a regular basis is a valuable one. Having such crucial information at your fingertips not only increases your confidence and efficiency, it also saves time.

◀ **Using PINs**
A PIN is one example of a number you cannot afford to forget.

STORING PINS AND PASSWORDS

If you can, make a PIN memorable, perhaps by using a familiar date, such as a relative's birthday. If you use a password and PIN together, use a word and number already related in your memory—for example, a friend's road and zip code. Alternatively, use the images from your Number System, and another that relates to the password. For a string of letters use the Phonetic Letter Technique. In all cases, make up a story that links the images and what you need to access—for example, an ATM.

Creating a Mental Notebook

Create different journeys for each day

⬇

Put images for tasks into each journey

⬇

As new tasks arise, add them to the end of the journey

⬇

Go over the journey in your mind several times a day

MEMORIZING DAY-TO-DAY JOBS

A mental notebook is useful for memorizing your tasks for the day. To plan ahead four or five days, use the Journey Technique and design four or five journeys. Using Image Creation Principles, make a mental image for each task, and insert it into the journey for that day. So if you have to pick up dry-cleaning, for example, you might imagine the clothes dancing around, accompanied by music and singing. If you have to do a task at a particular time, use your preferred Number System to add a number image. Start filling in your notebook two or three days ahead to fix it in your memory. If a new task arises, add it to the end of your journey. It is vital to review the tasks regularly—go through the journey in your head three times a day to ensure nothing is left out.

REMEMBERING DATES

To remember a date that crops up regularly, use your preferred Number System. For example, to remember April 19, use the images for the four digits 0419. To add a year, making six digits, such as 041966, use the technique for long numbers, splitting it into two three-digit numbers.

◀ **Memorizing special dates**
The Number Systems make it easy to recall an anniversary or birthday. Link the image for the date with an image for the person whose birthday or anniversary it is.

Choosing an Appropriate Technique

Type of Information	Recommended Memory Technique
Anniversaries, birthdays, PINs	Number Rhyme or Number Shape System
Passwords	Image Creation Principles
String of random letters	Phonetic Letter Technique

KEEPING A MENTAL PLANNER

Most people rely totally on a written or computerized planner for organizing their time on a monthly basis. Neither system is infallible, and you will find it very useful and time-efficient to have your planner with you, in your head, at all times. Learning your planner enables you to make immediate decisions when making appointments or other arrangements. The basis for a mental planner is the Journey Technique. Setting it up takes a little time initially, but once your system is in place, it is relatively simple to keep updated.

Transfers dates from calendar to mental planner

▲ **Setting up a mental planner**
Once you realize the benefits of having a mental diary with you wherever you are—and how it improves your efficiency—you will appreciate its advantages over, for example, wall calendars.

Useful Exercises

▶ Practice designing journeys with your family—it introduces them indirectly to memory skills.

▶ Put a calendar on the fridge door and look at the date when you get your breakfast. Go through what you have memorized for that day.

▶ Experiment with different journeys for your planner—then drop the ones that do not work well enough and use them for something else.

CREATING YOUR PLANNER

For a three-month planner, you need to create three journeys (one for each month), with one stage for each day of the month. To make it easier to find individual days within each journey, make definite breaks at stage 10 and stage 20. Use the three journeys in rotation. For each entry in the planner, create an image and insert it at the correct stage. So, for a dentist appointment on the 18th, for instance, your image might be a dentist drilling holes in his chair. Insert the image at the 18th stage. If you need to add a time, add the appropriate image from your Number System.

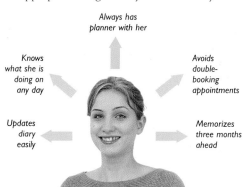

Always has planner with her

Knows what she is doing on any day

Avoids double-booking appointments

Updates diary easily

Memorizes three months ahead

◀ **Using a mental planner**
People who have set up a mental planner are efficient and reliable because they are able to check on appointments at any time, in any place. They can instantly call up any particular day or week to check entries or add in any new ones.

FOCUS POINTS

● Remember that it is important to learn the journeys really well before using them as a planner.

● Keep a constant eye open for places in which to create new journeys.

EXPANDING THE TECHNIQUE

If you find it easy to work with three journeys, you can increase the size of your planner and create more journeys, perhaps enough for six months or even for the whole year. You can keep the same imaginary routes year after year. Start each month with a significant image that denotes that month. If you are more comfortable using just three months at a time, you can write down dates that are more than three months ahead and insert them into a journey later.

Speaking in Public

Public speaking is a daunting prospect for many people. Learning how to memorize the key points of your speech or presentation—or even your part in a play—will enable you to deliver it to your audience in a natural and engaging manner.

> **"** It usually takes more than three weeks to prepare a good impromptu speech. **"**
>
> Mark Twain

▼ **Mind Mapping your speech**
Drawing this kind of map is a creative way to plan a speech, first identifying the main points and then adding in the detail.

PLANNING WHAT YOU WANT TO SAY

One of the best ways to write a speech or presentation is to Mind Map it. First write down the key words, and then add in all the related points that you wish to make. Using this method rather than writing out your speech word for word will make your delivery more natural. However, if you prefer to write your speech out in full, or at least in a more linear fashion, ensure you give it headings so that you can pick out key words.

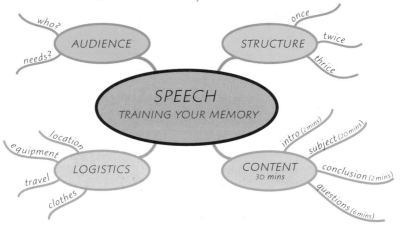

MEMORIZING A SPEECH

To memorize your speech or presentation, use the Journey Technique. This will also help you to time your delivery. For example, if you are planning to give a 20-minute speech without notes, find 20 key words and make a 20-stage journey. Take each of your key words, create an image for it, and insert one at each stage. If you wish to add extra details, such as statistics, use the images from your preferred Number System and add them the relevant stage. Practice the speech to make sure you are on target for the timing. Your speech will differ slightly each time you give it, which ensures that it sounds fresh.

▲ **Preparing your speech**
The key to a good speech is preparation. Rehearse it several times, perhaps in front of a mirror, until your delivery is natural.

| Choose key words | → | Create image for each key word | → | Put images into each stage of journey |

▲ **Making a presentation or speech**
The Journey Technique breaks your speech or presentation into stages. You can make one for each key point, or one for each minute you plan to speak.

LEARNING LINES AND QUOTATIONS

If you need to learn lines for a play, or to recite a poem or quotation, you can learn key words in a set order, as you would for a speech. However, since you must be word-perfect, you need to take this a stage further. Rehearse your lines using the Journey Technique to give you the main points and keep you on track. Then, to fix the finer points of the lines in your mind, you have to learn the words by repetition. If there are any areas you find hard to memorize, make sure you create images to help you remember them.

◀ **Learning by heart**
Actors can use the Journey Technique to memorize key words in the correct order. These trigger the rest of the lines, which are learned by heart.

Improving Skills

You can apply memory-training techniques to a wide range of skills that you use in day-to-day life, from absorbing information to playing sports and games, and learning a language. What is more, the learning experience is fun.

IMPROVING YOUR READING

Reading is something we all do—for work, for pleasure, or for study. Most of us, however, do not read as efficiently or effectively as we could, with the result that we do not retain in our memory as much of the material as we would like. One way to speed up your reading and make the material more memorable is to convert the book or article into a Mind Map. You will need to do this from the start, reading analytically, questioning the order and the hierarchy of the information. Organize the information in your mind, and then add it into your Mind Map.

◀ **Reading analytically**
Processing information as you read it will strongly improve your chances of understanding and then recalling it at a later date.

Things to Do

✓ Do try new things—chess, a foreign language, or a new sport. See how you can apply memory-training techniques.

✓ Do tell others what you are doing. You will feel good if you help someone else with their memory skills.

✓ Do have fun while learning. Enjoyment is the key to successful learning.

Things to Avoid

✗ Avoid doing too much at once. Use the techniques little and often at first.

✗ Avoid putting yourself under pressure with the techniques. Try them out at home on a personal level.

✗ Avoid learning for learning's sake. Apply the techniques to things that mean something to you.

MEMORIZING FACTS AND FIGURES

Being able to recall facts and figures improves your general knowledge—and is invaluable if you want to enter quizzes or competitions. Use the Association Technique to create an image out of each piece of information, then link them together. For example, if you want to remember that Michael Douglas won an Oscar in 1987, you would create an image for the number 1987 and attach it to Michael Douglas holding the Oscar statue. The important thing is to create an image that is memorable for you and therefore helps you to recall the associated information.

Fact File

Recall of new reading material is a huge problem for many people, simply because most printed matter—newspapers, business reports, and journals, as well as many books—consists mainly of black type on a white background. The best way to learn and remember anything is to follow the brain's natural way of working, which is to use the full spectrum of colors and innumerable different images.

Has mental image of an arm kept straight in splint

▲ **Applying imagination**
When you practice new techniques on the golf course, for example, the images you applied when you learned them will come into your head—perhaps a splint keeping your arm straight as you tee off

66 Imagination is more important than knowledge. Imagination encircles the world. 99

Albert Einstein

LEARNING A SPORT

Increasingly, time and attention are being devoted to the mental, as much as the physical, aspect of sporting performance. Memory skills are a great way to accelerate your learning, because they help you to develop good habits from the outset. When you are learning a new technique, such as a tennis stroke or golf swing, divide the technical aspects into key points. Create a simple, vivid image for each of these points. For example, if you need to keep your head still through your tennis serve, imagine that you are wearing a neck brace so your head is immobile. Create a journey (perhaps at your gym) in which to store the key points in order. When you start to play your game, the images for each point go through your mind.

PLAYING CHESS

Chess is a technical and strategic game. Opening and closing moves can be learned and applied, and previous games can be remembered as precedents for future games. To begin learning chess moves, you must first learn standard chess notation. Use the Journey Technique, the Phonetic Letter Technique, and your preferred Number System to learn these moves. Create a mental image for each move, design a journey, and insert the images into their respective stages. You may need a 50-stage journey for a full opening.

To memorize whether a move is black or white, mentally color your images black or white.

Useful Exercises

▶ Aim to learn one standard chess move each week for a month. Learn four more the next month, and so on.

▶ Keep your mind alert by playing fast-moving card games such as "War."

▶ Keep running through your 52 card images until you have achieved instant recall.

Uses Journey Technique to memorize moves

Colors images black or white

Starting out ▶
At the highest level, skill and inspiration play a great part in chess, but the novice can make big improvements by learning set moves.

FOCUS POINTS

● Memorizing cards is a wonderful social skill—especially for party tricks.

● Have confidence that your ability at cards will improve greatly—if you practice the techniques.

IMPROVING CARD SKILLS

Being able to memorize cards gives you an advantage in games, especially when you need to remember what has already been played. Use your Number System to create images for numbers one to 10. Picture cards have their own image, as does each suit. For each card make a composite image of the two components—so the three of clubs might be handcuffs swinging a golf club. To memorize the order of the pack, create a 52-stage journey, placing cards in the order they come out.

LEARNING A LANGUAGE

The method for learning vocabulary is founded on the same basis as the Association Technique used for remembering names. You can use this technique for words in any language; the important thing is to listen to the word and then create an association for it. Create an image from the sound of the foreign word, then attach that image to the word in your own language. For example, the German for newspaper is *die Zeitung*. To remember this, you might imagine someone you know named Simon (Si) with his tongue hanging out, reading a newspaper. To strengthen the image, visualize this scene at a newsstand.

▲ **Building up vocabulary**
Memory-training techniques can be used successfully to build a wide vocabulary—essential if you are to have the confidence to join in conversations in a foreign language, whether it be in a social or a business situation.

At a Glance

- A combination of memory-training techniques can help beginners at chess.
- A playing card can be memorized by making an image that combines suit and number.
- The order of a complete pack of cards can be memorized by using the Journey Technique.
- Foreign-language vocabulary can be quickly and easily built up through association.

> 66 The individual's whole experience is built upon the plan of his language. 99
>
> Henri Delacroix

GETTING TO GRIPS WITH GENDER

Some languages have more than one gender. There may be two genders—masculine and feminine; or three—masculine, feminine, and neuter. Gender is always crucial and has to be learned along with the vocabulary. The way to do this is to add a further dimension to your mental image of each word by coloring it according to its gender. You can choose your own colors for masculine, feminine, and neuter (if necessary), but you must stick to using the same ones all the time. As you learn each new word, mentally apply the relevant color to the image.

Adding color
You might choose blue for masculine words, red for feminine. Then, if the word "dog" is masculine, color it blue; if the word "door" is feminine, color it red.

Feminine

Masculine

Succeeding in Exams

Memory plays an important role in academic performance. An improved memory not only enhances your chances of doing well in exams, it gets your brain into good habits—the more effectively you learn, the more efficiently your memory works.

▼ **Studying for an exam**
Vary the techniques you use for studying. That way you keep up your interest—and go into the exam confident of full recall.

Recalls information quickly and accurately

USING MEMORY AIDS

There are different ways of approaching your studying to increase your recall of the information. Thirty percent of people are auditory learners—they prefer to use their hearing rather than reading ability. If you prefer to learn by listening, record some information on a tape or a minidisc. Play it back to yourself at different times of day—perhaps on a car journey or in bed, just before you go to sleep. Another technique is to use flash cards. Write questions on one side and answers on the other. You can give your cards to someone else to help you study, and you can use them to change the order in which you learn information; this will help your recall in an exam, when questions can be asked in any order.

Things to Do

✓ Do get used to the techniques by using a small amount of information at first.

✓ Do share the techniques with others studying the same subject as you.

✓ Do see how a technique can be used in a slightly different way for each subject.

Things to Avoid

✗ Avoid forcing your learning. If it feels like a serious chore, take a break.

✗ Avoid using just one type of learning tool—use them all.

✗ Avoid learning something of no interest to you, or you will have no motivation.

MEMORIZING LARGE AMOUNTS OF INFORMATION

The key to learning copious quantities of information is to reduce it down to manageable amounts. Mind Mapping does this by using key words. It also provides a way of organizing the information in a logical and comprehensive manner so that links and related information are apparent. You need to recall only the key words of your Mind Map—they will then automatically lead your mind on to relevant areas.

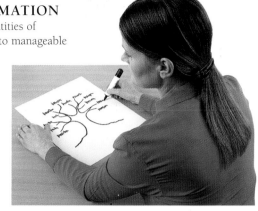

▲ **Making information manageable**
Mind Mapping is the best way to cope with large amounts of information. You might draw your Mind Map like a tree, writing key points on the main branches and then adding information of secondary importance on smaller branches, and so on.

66 Learning without thought is labor lost; thought without learning is perilous. 99

Confucius

Fact File

In many cases, when you are assimilating a large amount of information, you need to memorize only one word out of ten original words—your brain will be able to piece the rest together. Using Mind Mapping enables you to reduce a mass of information by up to 90 percent and yet maintain an excellent understanding of the subject matter.

MEMORIZING SETS OF FACTS

For a set of facts, such as a series of historical events, or the structure of a flower in biology, you can use the Journey Technique. If you were to use it to learn the nine planets in the solar system, for example, you would start by creating an image for each planet. So Mercury might be a thermometer, Earth might be an earth digger, and so on. Create a nine-stage journey, one stage for each planet. The location for your journey should be related to the subject matter, and should preferably be somewhere familiar—although, in this case, it might be aboard an imaginary spaceship. The next stage is to insert the images into the journey. You can then add any further information you want to learn at each stage, perhaps about the atmosphere, surface, or temperature of each planet.

Maintaining Retention and Recall

Up to 80 percent of all information learned is lost within 24 hours. *Reviewing information is crucial to high retention and good recall. If you do this at the correct times, you reduce the total number of reviews required.*

FOCUS POINT

● Review new information regularly—once or twice is not enough to commit it to long-term memory.

REVIEWING INFORMATION

To maximize learning you must review the new information before the level of recall drops too far. In the first 24 hours, the brain is playing with the new information, connecting it with existing information. This means it is relatively easy to recall during that period. Once this process is finished, the level of recall quickly drops. To prevent this from happening, you must review information regularly. This ensures that the brain continues to access the new information, assessing it and recalling it in detail.

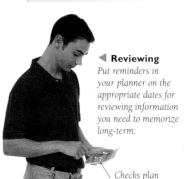

◀ **Reviewing**
Put reminders in your planner on the appropriate dates for reviewing information you need to memorize long-term.

Checks plan on PDA

At a Glance

● Most new information is lost within one day if you do not go over it an hour after learning it.

● Only by reviewing at regular intervals will you maintain long-term recall.

● As you become proficient at memorizing and recalling, you will feel confident enough to set new targets.

MAKING A PLAN

A written plan ensures that you consolidate your learning by recalling information at regular intervals. This is especially important for studying, but is essential for any information that you wish to retain long-term. The best time to review information is one hour after the initial learning. You should then review it a day after the initial learning, then a week, then a month, then three months, and finally every six months afterward. Mark these dates in your planner and make them part of your personal action plan.

SETTING NEW GOALS

Maintaining high recall builds your confidence in your memory, which in turn encourages you to continue your learning path. As memory techniques become a part of your life, you can use quiet times to review information or memorize new information. This will become a habit rather than a chore. As you devote more time to memorizing and recalling, you will want take on new challenges. When you set these higher goals, you can update your personal action plan.

Writes new goal into action plan

Updating your action plan ▶
As you become more efficient at memorizing, you will find yourself ready to set new targets. Review your action plan accordingly.

THE PATTERN OF RECALL

The graph shows your learning pattern and the best times to review new information. The first curved line shows recall immediately after learning. It starts at 80 percent and rises because the brain is associating the new information with data it already has. However, without a review, recall then drops quickly to about 20 percent. So, a review is necessary before recall drops below 80 percent, i.e., after one hour. The second line shows recall after the first review, a day later. Recall stays at about 40 percent unless it is reviewed again, a week later. With reviews at one, three, and six months, it stays at about 80 percent.

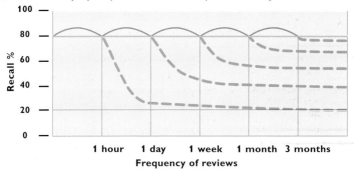

Recall %

100 — 80 — 60 — 40 — 20 — 0 —

1 hour   1 day   1 week   1 month   3 months

Frequency of reviews

Using Memory Aids

There are times when information cannot easily be committed to memory, and times when it has to be shared with others. Then memory aids come into their own. They are especially useful when used in conjunction with memory techniques.

WRITING LISTS

Lists are part of everyday life for many people. They can be used simply to make sure you do not forget some important item, or to help you organize work or leisure activities for the day, week, or month ahead. Apart from helping you feel in control of your life, the process of writing a list in itself aids your memory. Often writing something down is enough to commit it to memory.

Self-Talk

If you find yourself worrying that you have too much to do and might forget something important, try wording some statements like these and repeating them to yourself regularly to keep things on the right track.

"I have plenty of resources that I can rely on to remind me of appointments."

"I can enlist the help of my family to keep us organized."

"Putting some order into my life will help me feel in control."

▲ **Keeping long-term lists**
A permanent list of things you need to pack for a vacation is a time-efficient way of making sure you remember everything.

REUSING LISTS

Some lists can be used again and again, year after year. A good example is a vacation list, on which you write down all the things you need to take with you. This can save time and anxiety in the often frantic hours before you set off, and can prevent irritation when you get to your destination only to find you forgot to pack the insect repellent. Keep lists you are going to reuse in a safe place. For example, you might keep your vacation list in a notebook, along with the names and addresses that you need when you come to write your postcards. Any type of list, memorized or written, can lose its value if you do not keep it up to date. Reviewing lists of things on a regular basis, adding or deleting items as necessary, ensures that you continue to make use of the list.

◀ **Storing vital information**
A well-maintained personal organizer can put structure into your life.

RECORDING THINGS ON PAPER

A household address book is an excellent way of keeping and maintaining crucial information, when other members of the household need to access it. Planners and personal organizers can combine the functions of an address book and a notebook, as well being a good way of keeping track of birthdays, anniversaries, meetings, and dentist appointments.

ORGANIZING INFORMATION

An essential way of keeping on top of things at home is an efficient filing system. If this is used in conjunction with your planner or personal organizer, it can act as a reminder for things like quarterly bills or car servicing. A logical structure in your filing system is essential, perhaps alphabetically, by date, or by theme. Some people use separate boxes for household bills, the car, and so on. If you have a "Pending" file, look through it regularly.

▼ **Maintaining order**
Well-organized people are— and feel—consistently in control of their lives. They are efficient, get jobs done on time, and always remember important dates and appointments.

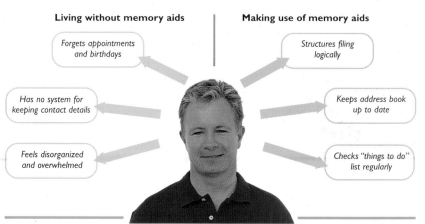

Living without memory aids

Forgets appointments and birthdays

Has no system for keeping contact details

Feels disorganized and overwhelmed

Making use of memory aids

Structures filing logically

Keeps address book up to date

Checks "things to do" list regularly

SHARING INFORMATION

When more than one person needs access to information, it is usually best to have it written down in some form. In the office, a wall-mounted, wipe-clean board is an invaluable way of reminding your team of schedules and tasks. As well as tracking progress, the board acts as a focus and helps to build team rapport. In the home, notes stuck on the fridge or a bulletin board help to keep families organized. A family calendar, on which all members of the family write their social engagements or extracurricular activities, makes it an easy matter to arrange time together as a family. It also teaches younger members to take responsibility for their lives.

Takes day off with family

Keeps space in calendar for outings

Keeping informed ▶
A communal calendar keeps everyone up to date with individual commitments as well as such occasions as a family outing.

KEEPING RECORDS

It is very easy to forget precisely what is said in meetings. Sometimes minutes are taken, but if no official record is being kept, make your own notes. Write clearly, so you can read your notes later. Some people find a small tape recorder or dictaphone is useful, but you should ask permission before you use it.

Taking notes ▶
It is always useful to take notes at a meeting, both as a record of what was said and as a reminder of things to be done.

MAKING USE OF DIGITAL REMINDERS

Computer software for keeping names and addresses, meeting reminders, and much else is widely available, and may even be included free in some operating systems. You can set up many of the programs so that they alert you to future appointments. The electronic, on-screen equivalents of paper "stickies" are useful. They have the advantage of not coming unstuck, with the loss of your precious lists and reminders.

Useful Exercises

▶ Look at the family calendar or planner over breakfast every morning to remind everyone of what they are doing that day.

▶ Make a Mind Map whenever you are planning with others, whether for a meeting at work or a family vacation. It will help all those involved plan better and remember the details longer.

▶ Keep paper and pencil by your bed and, before you go to sleep each night, write a list of things to do the next day. You will fall asleep feeling you have things under control.

▲ **Using electronic aids**
Laptop computers and handheld devices can transform the way we organize our lives. For example, you can check up on meetings and appointments at work and plan the week ahead from the comfort of your armchair.

USING ELECTRONIC ORGANIZERS

Most of us have computers at work or at home. These can be excellent ways of storing lists, calendars, and other memory aids. Handheld machines, often called PDAs (Personal Digital Assistants) can replace all the functions of paper-based systems, and have the advantage that you can work on them while traveling or away from the office or home, moving or copying the information from one machine to another. It is wise to keep copies of your files on your desktop computer, in case your PDA breaks or is stolen.

At a Glance

● A large noticeboard is useful for keeping a project team up to date with progress.

● A daybook kept at work is invaluable for future reference.

● Computers can be set up to alert you to forthcoming appointments.

● Names, addresses, and phone numbers can usefully be stored on your computer.

Keeping Your Memory Active

Exercising your brain and keeping your memory active increases the strength of your memory as you get older. You will find you are able to do things in later life you might never have considered, such as learning a language or a musical instrument.

DOING CROSSWORDS AND WORD GAMES

Exercises that keep your memory and brain active are those that require some mental effort. Crosswords and word games are excellent, because they push you to recall words that you might not use regularly. This encourages you to use them more often, so making you more articulate. You can also stretch yourself mentally by buying a book or a newspaper in a familiar foreign language. Reading it will make you think hard about any words you do not understand.

▲ **Maintaining mental agility**
Make use of a daily newspaper to stretch your brain—get in the habit of doing the crossword, or try translating some passages into another language.

Useful Exercises

▶ Play word games with your children. It will help stretch them in a fun way while keeping you on your toes.

▶ Learn to play a musical instrument. This uses many parts of the brain—and is also rewarding.

▶ Practice mental arithmetic when you are stuck in traffic or waiting for a bus.

USING MENTAL ARITHMETIC

Train yourself to do simple arithmetic in your head whenever the opportunity arises. You could add up the cost of the items in your grocery cart before you get to the checkout, for example, or you could try dividing a restaurant check between several people in your head. You can always confirm the results on a calculator, but as your mind becomes more efficient at simple arithmetic, you will learn to rely on it rather than the calculator. This keeps your short-term memory agile and your brain exercised.

KEEPING YOUR INTERESTS ALIVE

Apply the memory skills you are developing to things that interest you. If you are learning to play chess, for example, join your local club. If you are learning how to memorize cards, join a bridge club and try applying the techniques to your game. Expand the range of material you are learning by keeping up to date with developing technologies. The Internet, in particular, can open up a whole new world of information. Constant learning keeps your memory active, drip-feeding it new information to assimilate. Reading is a key part of this process, so read as often as you can. Vary the type of books and journals you read, and cover as wide a range of material as possible. You are always more likely to recall information that interests you than information that you find dull and boring, but every now and again try to read something in a new area to increase the scope of your memory and interests.

Uses Internet to research a topic

Emails interesting website to friend

Case Study

NAME: Richard
ISSUE: Losing mental agility
OBJECTIVE: To keep mind active

Richard is concerned that he is slowing down mentally. He has no interests outside his job, and colleagues find he has little conversation. He hears about the importance of keeping the brain active and takes action. He begins by buying a daily newspaper. He finds articles that interest him, and every evening uses the Internet to research the topic further. He does the crossword at lunchtime. He buys a book on one of the subjects that he has become interested in, and finds that reading stimulates and stretches his mind. Richard has now joined a reading group. He reads a new book every month, and is broadening his range of interests.

◄ Using the Internet

The Internet is a wonderful resource. It is an invaluable research tool for people of all ages, and there is no end to the information available on innumerable topics. Many people find using email enables them to share interests with friends all over the world.

Assessing Your Memory

*N*ow that you have read this book, respond to the following statements by marking the answers that are closest to your experience. Be as honest as you can: if your answer is "Never," mark Option 1; if it is "Always," mark Option 4; and so on. Add up your scores, and refer to the analysis to see how you feel about your memory now.

Options

1 Never
2 Occasionally
3 Frequently
4 Always

How Do You Respond?

	1	2	3	4
1 I believe anyone can improve their memory.	☐	☐	☐	☐
2 I know I can develop my memory's potential.	☐	☐	☐	☐
3 I believe memory need not worsen with age.	☐	☐	☐	☐
4 I know I can develop my short-term memory.	☐	☐	☐	☐
5 I know I can improve my long-term memory.	☐	☐	☐	☐
6 I am capable of learning and recalling names.	☐	☐	☐	☐
7 Studying can be fun and effective.	☐	☐	☐	☐
8 I eat a balanced and healthy diet.	☐	☐	☐	☐
9 I follow a regular exercise program.	☐	☐	☐	☐

	1	2	3	4
10 My sleep quality is good.	☐	☐	☐	☐
11 I trust my memory.	☐	☐	☐	☐
12 My outlook on life is positive.	☐	☐	☐	☐
13 I believe I can be as creative as I wish.	☐	☐	☐	☐
14 Goal-setting is part of my daily routine.	☐	☐	☐	☐
15 My concentration is good.	☐	☐	☐	☐
16 I keep my life well-ordered.	☐	☐	☐	☐
17 I have a multisensory approach to learning.	☐	☐	☐	☐
18 I remember words without difficulty.	☐	☐	☐	☐

	1	2	3	4
19 I look for patterns in information.	☐	☐	☐	☐
20 I memorize lists accurately.	☐	☐	☐	☐
21 I draw Mind Maps.	☐	☐	☐	☐
22 I can memorize a series of digits.	☐	☐	☐	☐
23 Remembering times and dates is easy.	☐	☐	☐	☐
24 I do mental arithmetic with ease.	☐	☐	☐	☐
25 I speak in public without notes.	☐	☐	☐	☐

	1	2	3	4
26 I enjoy learning new skills.	☐	☐	☐	☐
27 I feel confident I can learn a new language.	☐	☐	☐	☐
28 I review information to improve recall.	☐	☐	☐	☐
29 I learn with friends and family.	☐	☐	☐	☐
30 I do mentally stimulating exercises.	☐	☐	☐	☐
31 I am confident about memory techniques.	☐	☐	☐	☐
32 I am excited about the power of my memory.	☐	☐	☐	☐

Analysis

When you have added up your scores, look at the analysis below. Note the areas where you perform well and areas where you still need to improve. Compare scores with those on your initial assessment on pages 16–17 to see how far you have come.

32–64 You are having difficulty adjusting your approach to memory skills and, to develop your memory's potential, you need to work hard on the techniques.

65–95 Your attitude and your memory's performance are good. But there is still work to be done on your skills.

96–128 Congratulations! Your memory performance is very good indeed. All you need to do is keep practicing your skills.

My weakest areas are:

_____

_____

_____

_____

My strongest areas are:

_____

_____

_____

_____

Index

Acknowledgments

AUTHOR'S ACKNOWLEDGMENTS

Julie, Danielle, and Nathan for showing me how to be a better human being.

Mind Maps® are the trademark of Tony Buzan. For further information, contact Buzan Centres Ltd., 54 Parkstone Road, Poole, Dorset BH15 2PX, U.K.

PUBLISHER'S ACKNOWLEDGMENTS

Dorling Kindersley would like to thank the following for their help and participation:

Design Assistant Dennis Buckley; **Editorial Assistant** Laura Seber;
Design Consultant Laura Watson; **Editorial Consultant** Kate Hayward;
Jacket Designer John Dinsdale; **Jacket Editor** Jane Oliver-Jedrzejak
Indexer Hilary Bird; **Proofreader** John Sturges; **Photography** Steve Gorton

Models Angela Cameron, Kuo Kang Chen, Mei Lien Chen, Jan Davidson, Hannah Fuller, Philip Holloway, Tom Jennings, Kathleen McMahon, Cameron Moss, Marilyn Reynolds, Laura Seber, Nick Sherlock, John Sturges; **Make-up** Carolyn Boult

Picture research by Ilumi; **Picture librarian** Lucy Claxton

PICTURE CREDITS

The publisher would like to thank the following for their kind permission to reproduce their photographs:

Key: *a*=above; *b*=bottom; *c*=center; *l*=left; *r*=right; *t*=top
Arena images: 53b; **Corbis:** Ed Bock, 44b; Stewart Cohen, 62; Jim Cummins, 22; Mark A. Johnson, 20t; Araldo de Luca, 38; Ariel Shelly, 4/5; George Shelley, 48; Corey Sorensen, 54;
Getty Images: David Boissavy/Taxi, 31t; Digital Vision, 37t;
Bruce Laurance, 66; David Oliver/Taxi, 27; Anderson Ross/Photodisc, 14.

All other images © Dorling Kindersley
For further information see: www.dkimages.comcom

AUTHOR'S BIOGRAPHY

David Thomas is an international professional speaker, international media personality, businesssman and one of the world's most powerful memorizers. He is an International Grandmaster of Memory, a World Memory Championships medallist and *Guinness Book of Records* memory record holder. On May 1, 1998, he recited the mathematical formula Pi (3.14159…) to 22,500 digits from memory without error. He has appeared in over 100 media interviews in countries as far afield as Great Britain, South Africa, Canada, the United States, and Bermuda.